Peace on Earth,
& Merry Christmas!

2018

THIS SHALL BE A SIGN
The Nativity of Jesus Christ

Antonio Allegri da Correggio
Adoration of the Shepherds

Stephen R. Capps

ISBN 978-1-64114-079-9 (hardcover)
ISBN 978-1-64114-078-2 (digital)

Christian Faith Publishing, Inc.M
832 Park Avenue
Meadville, PA 16335
www.christianfaithpublishing.com

"Adoration of the Magi"

Bartolomé Esteban Murillo

Printed in the United States of America

The story of the Nativity seamlessly woven from the four Gospel narratives and Old Testament prophecies, preserving the elegant language of the King James Version of the Holy Bible, and illustrated with selected works of seventeenth-, eighteenth-, and nineteenth-century artists.

Dedication

To the women in my life:

my loving wife, who has believed in me from the beginning;

my two beautiful daughters, who are so
passionate about everything they do;

my wonderful sisters, who have always been there for me;

and my mother, who taught me to believe.

Preface

A few years ago I found myself trying to assemble the Christmas story from the New Testament to share with my family. A few things made this task more complicated than I had anticipated.

First, the narrative is scattered not only across the four Gospels, but also reaches back into the Old Testament in a number of instances. The accounts also overlap in time, and there is some repetition between them, but each contributes detail that enriches the whole.

Second, the narrative styles found in the Gospel accounts differ from one another, sometimes considerably. As a result, even when I finally managed to stitch the story of the nativity of Jesus Christ together chronologically, the text was inconsistent and choppy.

I decided I would attempt to render my patchwork version in a single voice while trying to preserve the spirit of the original Gospel accounts. While I do not pretend to have improved upon the original, I'd like to think that I have succeeded in my endeavor to some extent, and made the story of the events surrounding the birth of the Savior a bit more accessible.

It was not easy, in many cases, to decide which works of art to use in illustrating this book. The ones I've chosen are not only beautiful, but also offer powerful evidence of the influence that Jesus Christ has had on our entire civilization.

If I am honest with myself, I cannot in good conscience claim to be the author of this book, and I am certainly not the illustrator. For that you have many great scholars and talented artists to thank. My role in the creation of this book has been more that of an editor. I hope you will feel, with me, the wonder and majesty that these words and works convey, as well as the love that these scholars and artists felt for Jesus Christ, who truly was Lord at his birth.

Introduction

(Luke 1:1–3; 2 Peter 1:15–16)

In this latter day, it seems prudent
and entirely necessary to assemble and set forth
the account of the nativity of Jesus Christ
which is still believed among his followers;
for we do not follow cunningly devised fables
as to the birth of our Lord,
but rather desire to confirm once again unto the world
those things which were foretold by the prophets
and testified to by those who were called
to bear witness and had perfect understanding,
that we all might be reminded of their certainty,
to the encouragement and confirmation of our faith.

An Angel Appears to Zacharias

(Luke 1:5–25)

James Tissot
Zacharias and Elizabeth

In the days of Herod, the king of Judæa, there lived a certain priest named Zacharias with his wife Elisabeth. They were both righteous, walking blameless in all the commandments and ordinances of the Lord; yet they had no child because Elisabeth was barren, and they were both well stricken in years.

And it came to pass that Zacharias, in the execution of his priestly office, went into the temple to burn incense before God, while without the whole multitude of the people were praying.

Rembrandt
Zacharias and the Angel

And an angel of the Lord appeared, standing on the right side of the altar of incense; and when Zacharias saw him, he was troubled, and fear fell upon him.

And the angel said unto him, "Fear not, Zacharias: for thy prayer is heard; and thy wife Elisabeth shall bear thee a son, and thou shalt call his name John. He shall be great in the sight of the Lord, and shall be filled with the Holy Ghost, even from his mother's womb. And he shall turn the hearts of the fathers to the children, and many of the children of Israel to the Lord their God, to make ready a people prepared for the Lord."

Image courtesy of Bizzell
Bible Collection
*University of Oklahoma
Libraries*

William Blake
Zacharias and the Angel

And Zacharias said unto the angel, "Whereby shall I know this? I am an old man, and my wife well stricken in years."

And the angel answering said, "I am Gabriel, that stands in the presence of God; and I am sent to shew thee these glad tidings. And because thou believest not my words, which shall be fulfilled in their season, behold, thou shalt not be able to speak until the day that these things shall be performed."

And the people waited and marveled that Zacharias tarried so long in the temple.

Seventeenth-century etching
*Zacharias Gestures to the People
that He Has Had a Vision*

And when he came out, he beckoned unto them and remained speechless. And the people perceived that he had seen a vision.

And it came to pass that after the days of his ministration in the temple were accomplished, Zacharias departed to his own house. And Elisabeth conceived, and said, "Thus hath the Lord dealt with me, to take away my reproach among men."

The Angel Salutes Mary

(Luke 1:26–38)

Henry Ossawa Tanner
The Annunciation

And it came to pass that the angel Gabriel was also sent from God to the city of Nazareth in Galilee, to a virgin espoused to a man of the house of David whose name was Joseph; and the virgin's name was Mary.

And Gabriel came to her and said, "Hail, thou that art highly favored! The Lord is with thee! Blessed art thou among women!"

Francisco Goya
The Annunciation

And Mary was troubled when she saw him and cast in her mind what manner of salutation this should be. And Gabriel said unto her, "Fear not, for thou hast found favor with God. Behold, thou shalt conceive, and bring forth a son, and shalt call his name Jesus. He shall be called the Son of the Highest, and the Lord God shall give unto him the throne of his father David. Of his kingdom there shall be no end, and he shall reign over the house of Jacob forever."

Then Mary said unto the angel, "How shall this be, seeing I know not a man?"

Then answered the angel Gabriel, "The Holy Ghost shall come upon thee, and the power of the Highest shall overshadow thee: therefore that holy thing which shall be born of thee shall be called the Son of God."

And Mary said, "Behold the handmaid of the Lord; be it unto me according to thy word."

And Gabriel also proclaimed to Mary, "Behold, thy cousin Elisabeth hath also conceived a son in her old age: and this is the sixth month with her, who was called barren. For with God nothing shall be impossible."

Mary Visits Her Cousin Elisabeth

(Luke 1:39–56)

And after the angel departed from her, Mary arose and went with haste into the hill country and entered into the house of Zacharias, and she saluted Elisabeth.

And it came to pass that when Elisabeth, who was in her sixth month, heard the salutation of Mary, the babe leaped in her womb; and Elisabeth was filled with the Holy Ghost, and spake out with a loud voice, "Blessed art thou

Carl Heinrich Bloch
Mary's Visit to Elizabeth

among women, and blessed is the fruit of thy womb! And whence is the mother of my Lord come to me?

"Lo, as soon as thy voice sounded in mine ears, the babe leaped in my womb for joy. Blessed is she that believed: for there shall be a performance of those things which were told her from the Lord."

And Mary said, "My soul doth magnify the Lord, and my spirit hath rejoiced in God my Savior; for he hath

Anton Franz Maulbertsch Fresco in the cathedral in Vác, Hungary
The Song of Mary (detail)

Robert Anning Bell
Mary in the House of Elizabeth

regarded the low estate of his hand-maiden: for henceforth all genera-tions shall call me blessed, for he that is mighty hath done to me great things. Holy is his name, and his mercy is on them that fear him from generation to generation. He hath scattered the proud in the imagina-tion of their hearts. He hath put down the mighty, and exalted them of low degree. He hath filled the hungry; and the rich he hath sent empty away. He hath remembered Israel in mercy, as he spake to Abraham, and to his seed forever."

So Mary abode with Elisabeth for about three months, and then she returned to her own house.

Elizabeth Gives Birth

(Luke 1:57–80; Isaiah 40:3)

Now Elisabeth's full time came that she should be delivered; and she brought forth a son. And her neighbors and cousins heard how the Lord had shewed great mercy upon her; and they rejoiced with her.

Domenico Ghirlandaio
Birth of St. John the Baptist

And on the eighth day they came to circumcise the child; and they called him Zacharias, after the name of his father.

Julius Schnorr von Carolsfeld
His Name Is John

And Elisabeth answered and said, "Not so; but he shall be called John." And they said unto her, "There is none of thy kindred that is called by this name."

And they made signs to his father, how he would have him called. And he asked for a writing tablet, and wrote, saying, "His name is John." And they all marveled.

And the mouth of Zacharias was opened immediately, and his tongue loosed, and being filled with the Holy Ghost, he prophesied, saying, "Blessed be the Lord God of Israel! For as he spake by the mouth of his holy prophets which have been since the world began, he hath visited and redeemed his people and hath raised up an horn of salvation

Jacopo Tintoretto
The Birth of John the Baptist (detail)

for us in the house of David, that we should be saved from our enemies and from the hand of all that hate us, to perform the mercy promised to our fathers, and to remember his holy covenant, and the oath which he sware to our father Abraham, that we might serve him without fear, in holiness and righteousness, all the days of our life.

"And thou, child, shalt be called the prophet of the Highest: for thou shalt go before the face of the Lord to prepare his ways; to give knowledge of salvation unto his people by the remission of their sins, through the tender mercy of our God; whereby the dayspring from on high hath visited us, to give light to them that sit in darkness and in the shadow of death, to guide our feet into the way of peace."

And fear came on all that dwelt round about them: and all these sayings were noised abroad throughout all the hill country of Judæa. And all they that heard them laid them up in their hearts, saying, "What manner of child shall this be?"

This was he of whom Isaiah prophesied, saying that his would be the voice of one "that crieth in the wilderness, Prepare ye the way of the Lord, make straight in the desert a highway for our God."

An Angel Reassures Joseph

(Matthew 1:18–25; Isaiah 7:14–15)

Now before Mary and Joseph came together, she was found to be with child of the Holy Ghost. Then Joseph, being a just man, and not willing to make her a public example, was minded to put her away privily.

But while he thought on these things, behold, the angel of the Lord appeared unto him in a dream, saying, "Joseph, thou son of David,

Gaetano Gandolfi
Joseph's Dream

fear not to take unto thee Mary thy wife: for that which is conceived in her is of the Holy Ghost. And she shall bring forth a son, and thou shalt call his name Jesus: for he shall save his people from their sins."

Schelte à Bolswert
The Marriage of Joseph and Mary
(detail)

Then Joseph being raised from sleep did as the angel of the Lord had bidden him, and took unto him his wife, and knew her not till she had brought forth the child.

All this was done, that it might be fulfilled which was spoken of the Lord by the prophet Isaiah, saying, "The Lord himself shall give you a sign; Behold, a virgin shall conceive, and bear a son, and shall call his name Immanuel—which being interpreted is, God with us. Butter and honey shall he eat, that he may know to refuse the evil, and choose the good."

The Birth of Jesus Christ

(Luke 2:1–7; Matthew 1:18–25; Isaiah 9:2, 6–7)

And it came to pass in those days, a decree went out from Cæsar Augustus that all the world should be taxed; and all went to be taxed, every one into his own city.

And Joseph, because he was of the house and lineage of David, went up out of Nazareth into Judæa, unto the city of David which is called Bethlehem, to be taxed with Mary his wife, being great with child.

William Brassey Hole
Joseph and Mary Arrive at Bethlehem

Now the birth of Jesus Christ was on this wise: when Joseph and Mary arrived in Bethlehem, there was no room for them in the inn. And so it was, when the days were accomplished that Mary should be delivered, she brought forth her firstborn son, and wrapped him in swaddling clothes and laid him in a manger; and they called his name Jesus.

Gerard van Honthorst
Adoration of the Shepherds
(detail)

This was the very child spoken of by the prophet Isaiah when he declared, "The people that walked in darkness have seen a great light: they that dwell in the land of the shadow of death, upon them hath the light shined. For unto us a child is born, unto us a son is given: and the government shall be upon his shoulder: and his name shall be called Wonderful, Counsellor, The mighty God, The everlasting Father, The Prince of Peace. Of the increase of his government and peace there shall be no end, upon the throne of David, and upon his kingdom, to order it, and to establish it with judgment and with justice from henceforth even forever. The zeal of the Lord of hosts will perform this."

Angels Proclaim the Birth to Shepherds

(Luke 2:8-20)

And in that same country were shepherds abiding in the field, keeping watch over their flock by night. And, lo, the angel of the Lord came upon them, and the glory of the Lord shone round about them: and they were sore afraid.

Carl Bloch
Shepherds Abiding in the Fields

And the angel said unto them, "Fear not: for, behold, I bring you good tidings of great joy, which shall be to all people; for unto you is born this day in

29

the city of David a Savior, which is Christ the Lord. And this shall be a sign unto you; Ye shall find the babe wrapped in swaddling clothes, lying in a manger."

And suddenly there was with the angel a multitude of the heavenly host praising God, and saying, "Glory to God in the highest, and on earth peace, good will toward men!"

And it came to pass, as the angels were gone away from them into heaven, the shepherds said one to another, "Let us now go even unto Bethlehem, and see this thing which is come to pass, which the Lord hath made known unto us."

Rembrandt
The Angel Appearing to the Shepherds
(detail)

And they came with haste, and found Mary, and Joseph, and the babe lying in a manger.

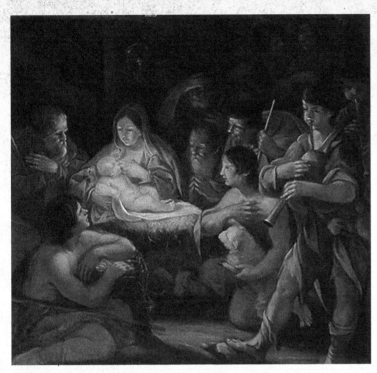

Guido Reni
The Adoration of the Shepherds (detail)

And when they had seen it, the shepherds made known abroad the saying which was told them concerning this child. And all they that heard it wondered at those things which were told them by the shepherds; but Mary kept all these things, and pondered them in her heart.

And the shepherds returned, glorifying and praising God for all the things that they had heard and seen, as it was told unto them.

Joseph and Mary Present Jesus in the Temple

(Luke 2:22–39)

And when eight days were accomplished for the circumcising of the child, his name was called Jesus, as he was so named by the angel before he was conceived in the womb.

Pieter-Jozef Verhaghen
The Presentation in the Temple

And when, according to the law of Moses, the days of Mary's purification were accomplished, they brought Jesus to Jerusalem, to present him to the Lord, and to offer a sacrifice according to the law of the Lord.

Rembrandt van Rijn
The Hymn of Simeon

And, behold, in Jerusalem lived a man whose name was Simeon, a just and devout man, who waited for the consolation of Israel, to whom it had been revealed by the Holy Ghost that he should not see death before he had seen the Lord's Christ. And he came by the Spirit into the temple.

And when Mary and Joseph brought the child Jesus in, to do for him after the custom of the law, the Holy Ghost was upon Simeon, and he took Jesus up in his arms, and blessed God, and said, "Lord, now let thou thy servant depart in peace, for according to thy word mine eyes have seen thy salvation, which thou hast prepared before the face of all people; a light to lighten the Gentiles, and the glory of thy people Israel!"

And when Joseph and Mary marveled at those things which were spoken of Jesus, Simeon blessed them, and said unto his mother, "Behold, this child is set for the fall and rising again of many in Israel; and for a sign which shall be spoken against, that the thoughts of many hearts may be revealed; yea, and a sword shall pierce through thy own soul also."

Rembrandt van Rijn
The Presentation of Jesus in the Temple

And one Anna, a prophetess of a great age, also served God in the temple with fasting and prayer night and day; and she, coming in at that instant, likewise gave thanks unto the Lord, and she spake of Jesus to all them that looked for redemption in Jerusalem.

And when Joseph and Mary had performed all things according to the law of the Lord, they returned to their own city of Nazareth in Galilee.

Wise Men Seek the Christ Child

Matthew 2:1–11; Micah 5:2

Now in the days after the birth of Jesus in Bethlehem of Judæa, behold, there came wise men from the east to Jerusalem, saying, "Where is he that is born King of the Jews? For we have seen his star in the east, and are come to worship him."

James Tissot
The Journey of the Magi

And when Herod the king had heard these things, he was troubled, and all Jerusalem with him.

And he had gathered all the chief priests and scribes of the people together, and demanded of them where Christ should be born. And they said unto him, "In Bethlehem of Judæa, for thus it is written by the prophet, Micah:

James Tissot
Three Wise Men

'But thou, Bethlehem Ephratah, though thou be little among the thousands of Judah, yet out of thee shall he come forth unto me that is to be ruler in Israel.'"

Then when Herod had privily called the wise men, he enquired of them diligently what time the star appeared, and said, "Go and search diligently for the young child; and when ye have found him, bring me word again, that I may come and worship him also," and he sent them to Bethlehem.

Gustave Dore
Wise Men Guided by the Star

When they had heard the king, the wise men departed; and, lo, the star which they saw in the east, went before them, till it came and stood over where the young child was. When they saw the star, they rejoiced with exceeding great joy.

Matthias Stom
Adoration of the Magi

And when the wise men were come into the house, they saw the young child with Mary his mother, and fell down, and worshipped him: and when they had opened their treasures, they presented unto him gifts; gold, and frankincense, and myrrh.

And the wise men, being warned of God in a dream that they should not return to Herod, departed into their own country another way.

Henry Osawa Tanner
The Three Wise Men

Joseph and Mary Flee
with Jesus into Egypt

(Matthew 2:13–23; Jeremiah 31:15)

And, behold, the angel of the Lord appeared to Joseph in a dream, saying, "Arise, and take the young child and his mother, and flee into Egypt, and be thou there until I bring thee word: for Herod will seek the young child to destroy him."

Henry Osawa Tanner
Flight into Egypt

So when Joseph arose, he took the young child Jesus and Mary his mother by night, and departed into Egypt.

And when Herod saw that he was mocked of the wise men, he was exceeding wroth, and sent forth, and slew all the children that were in Bethlehem, and in all the coasts thereof, from two years old and under, according to the time which he had diligently enquired of the wise men.

Giovanni Battista Merano
Massacre of the Innocents

This fulfilled that which was spoken by Jeremiah the prophet, saying, "In Rama was there a voice heard, lamentation, and weeping, and great mourning, Rachel weeping for her children, and would not be comforted, because they are not."

Joseph and Mary Return with Young Jesus to Nazareth

(Matthew 2:19–23; Hosea 11:1)

So Joseph remained in Egypt with Jesus and Mary, until the death of Herod. Then, behold, an angel of the Lord again appeared in a dream to Joseph in Egypt, saying, "Arise, and take the young child and his mother, and go into the land of Israel: for they which sought the young child's life are dead," that it might be fulfilled which was

Bartolome Esteban Murillo
Dream

spoken of the Lord by the prophet Hosea, saying, "Out of Egypt have I called my son."

James Tissot
The Return from Egypt

And Joseph arose, and took the young child and his mother, and came into the land of Israel; but when he heard that Archelaus did reign in Judæa in the room of Herod his father, Joseph was afraid to go thither; and turned aside into the parts of Galilee: and came and dwelt in a city called Nazareth: that it might be fulfilled which was spoken by the prophets, "He shall be called a Nazarene."

And the child grew, and waxed strong in spirit, filled with wisdom: and the grace of God the Father was upon him.

John Everett Millais
Christ in the House of His Parents

About the Author

Stephen Capps has long dreamed of becoming a writer. As a family man with a full-time job and involvement in church service, he would often begin projects, both fiction and nonfiction, but never managed to carve out enough time to complete much of anything. Now that he's been retired for a few years, he has found more time to realize his dream.

On his retirement, instead of picking up a project that he had already started, he chose to write this book. While Stephen feels that fictional worlds may offer the opportunity to explore moral and ethical ideas from a Christian perspective in a creative way, his choice to focus initially on nonfiction reflects Stephen's desire, first and foremost, to bear a firm witness of his faith in the divinity of Jesus Christ and a literal interpretation of the scriptures.

In addition to spending more time writing and an ardent desire to share the gospel, Stephen's interests include reading, listening to classical music, genealogy, puzzles of all kinds, and keeping up with current events—especially anything related to science. He shares his daily life with his sweet wife. They are empty-nest parents of two beautiful and talented daughters, have a wonderful grandson, and are adoptive parents to a secondhand Shi Tzu.

CPSIA information can be obtained
at www.ICGtesting.com
Printed in the USA
BVHW02*1651140918
527379BV00003B/6/P